A MOTHER'S TESTIMONY *of* FAITH *and* PRAYER

YOU ARE STILL GOOD

LA'WANA HARRIS

Also by La'Wana Harris
Jaden Israel: The Prince of God
Jaden Israel: America by Train: The California Zephyr
America by Train: Yosemite National Park

Scripture quotations marked (ESV) are from the ESV® Bible
(The Holy Bible, English Standard Version®), copyright © 2001 by Crossway,
a publishing ministry of Good News Publishers. Used by permission. All rights reserved.

Scripture quotations are taken from the Holy Bible, New Living Translation,
copyright ©1996, 2004, 2007, 2013, 2015 by Tyndale House Foundation.
Used by permission of Tyndale House Publishers, Inc., Carol Stream, Illinois 60188.
All rights reserved.

Scripture taken from the Holy Bible, NEW INTERNATIONAL VERSION®, NIV®
Copyright © 1973, 1978, 1984, 2011 by Biblica, Inc.®
Used by permission. All rights reserved worldwide.

Scriptures marked KJV are taken from the KING JAMES VERSION (KJV):
KING JAMES VERSION, public domain.

"Scripture taken from the New King James Version.
Copyright © 1982 by Thomas Nelson, Inc. Used by permission. All rights reserved.

Scripture quotations taken from the New American Standard Bible® (NASB),
Copyright © 1960, 1962, 1963, 1968, 1971, 1972, 1973,
1975, 1977, 1995 by The Lockman Foundation
Used by permission. www.Lockman.org

© 2017 La'Wana Harris

No part of this publication may be reproduced or transmitted in any
form or by any means, electronic, mechanical, including photocopy,
recording, or any information storage and retrieval system, without
permission in writing from the author.

YOU ARE STILL GOOD

LA'WANA HARRIS

This book is dedicated to mothers who have welcomed children into the world and then faced the unthinkable task of watching one of their children leave this world.

To fathers who are the pillar of strength during times of difficulty for their families.

To all caregivers of children and loved ones that have faced tragedy or crisis situations.

To all who believe or want to believe in the healing power of Jesus Christ.

And to Almighty God who loves us more than we could ever comprehend.

Acknowledgements

I would like to thank the many people
who made this book possible:

To my wonderful husband
for his support and encouragement.

To my three beautiful children
who will forever be my greatest gifts.

To my mom, a prayer warrior
and faithful woman of God.

To Reverend Dick and Lonnie VanCleave,
who demonstrated the love of Christ
when we needed it most.

Introduction

Have you ever found yourself facing a crisis or tragic event that challenged your faith? Do you need encouragement to stand on God's word when circumstances do not align with what God has said? Did you really hear from God? What if things get worse after you declare God's word?

I just want to share my story as a mother, and hopefully give someone else some insight, encouragement, and inspiration that if they do find themselves in a crisis situation, they are not alone. My mission is to honor God, to inspire others, and to provide some tangible tools to the readers who might find themselves in similar situations.

When you are in a crisis situation, a lot of what you know sometimes just goes out the window because you are trying to process all that you are going through, even if you have been walking with the Lord a long time.

In these pages readers will see the benefits and challenges associated with standing firm when God reveals his will to them before it manifests in the natural.

I want mothers and fathers who share crisis experiences with their children to know that they are never alone, and that there is hope on the other side of tragedy. Come along with me as I testify to the power of prayer and trusting in God's word.

> *For our gospel did not come to you in word only, but also in power, and in the Holy Spirit and in much assurance* (1 Thessalonians 1:5) NKJV.

Contents

1. The Beginning of Our Journey — 15
2. Odd Behavior — 20
3. Things Change in an Instant — 25
4. Peace in the Midst of Crisis — 31
5. Confidence — 38
6. Comfort — 44
7. Believe and Obey — 47
8. All is Well — 52
9. Questions — 58
10. No One Gets the Glory but God! — 64
11. Rehab — 70
12. The Process — 75
13. Progress Begins — 81
14. Resuming School — 86
15. Graduation Day — 90

Epilogue — 93

Lessons Learned — 97

About the Author — 101

YOU ARE STILL GOOD

1

The Beginning of Our Journey

It was two days before Christmas and we were in the middle of our usual Harris Family Christmas traditions. The tree had been up for a few weeks already, following our family tradition of piling into the car and going together to pick out the perfect tree. The experience is always comical because my husband automatically goes to the largest one on the lot and declares it to be "the one," no matter that a nine foot tree absolutely does not fit our seven foot ceilings. We eventually go with his choice but heckle him a bit at home when he is forced to trim a few feet off the bottom of the tree to accommodate the star at the top.

The two older boys, Eddie and Malcolm, were home from college, the house was decorated, and everyone was spilling over with holiday cheer. (We are known for going a little over the top for the holidays.) Every year we cook a very traditional holiday meal while at the same time trying a few new dishes to expand our culinary experience. I travel a lot around the world for my work in leadership development and along the way collect spices and ingredients to use when we are all together. (We've tried everything from worms and crickets to exotic spices from Southeast Asia.)

My oldest son, Eddie II, or as we call him "Little Eddie," was helping me cook and get things organized. We all chuckle when we call him "Little Eddie," seeing that his strikingly handsome frame is now six feet tall and he has broad shoulders like a line backer. He is also a fabulous cook and is always looking to get his hands on my highly coveted secret ingredients.

As the eldest son he has always taken on the role of being the voice of reason with a very level headed approach to things when the rest of us are taking our holiday contests way too seriously. Growing up, like most first born children, he graciously assumed the responsibility of sharing in the care of his little brother and sister that comes with being the eldest child. *This sense of responsibility and his level headedness would very much be a great support in the days just ahead.*

Malcolm is the middle child and he was also home from college on the holiday break. He is the athlete of the family, following in his dad's footsteps. He played most sports growing up and has evolved into a handsome, smart young man. He stays fit and encourages us to do the same. Our home was never empty when he was around because many of his teammates would swoop in and raid the fridge. He is also the jokester of the family. We've always said that one of the gifts

God gave him was to make people laugh. *We would certainly need that gift too in the days and months ahead.*

Jasmine is the baby of the family and the only girl. So yes, she is a little spoiled. She is a natural beauty inside and out. I remember looking at her perfect almond brown skin with that little pug nose and falling helplessly in love with her the moment I saw her for the first time.

She is the natural born creative of the family. She can fashion just about anything she dreams up. People often tell her she has an eye for creating beautiful things by conceptualizing how things should come together. It has been quite remarkable to watch her talent blossom through the years.

Everyone fights to have Jasmine on their team whenever we have family contests that involve creativity. (These contests are a serious matter, and happen quite frequently due to the competitive and fun nature of the Harris gang!) She has always shown compassion for others from a very young age and loves to participate in humanitarian activities. *Little did we know how much compassion she herself would need in the coming days.*

My husband, "Big Eddie," could also be caricatured as "Steady Eddie" due to his desire to keep things in a very orderly fashion at all times. The two of us are like Felix and Oscar from the "The Odd Couple." He is reserved and observant—a text book introvert. He prefers to live a very simple, country life, enjoying down home southern cooking, fishing, and hanging out at home. He is the youngest of 20 children and I think because of that, nothing seems to throw him. *His steadiness would be such a blessing in the days ahead.*

In a nutshell, Little Eddie was cooking and keeping a level head while we were enjoying the holidays. Malcolm was impersonating folks, talking in several made up languages and accents, telling jokes, eating up all of the candy and sweets, sneaking into dishes that were to be saved for our formal dinner, playing practical jokes on all of us, and providing 24/7 top notch entertainment.

And Jasmine was planning her outfits, working with me to distribute toys and food to the less fortunate, and creating beautiful crafts to decorate the house. My husband was sitting in his recliner, directing the whole scene as if it were an action movie while making sure that all messes were promptly cleaned up.

And me? I was running around blissfully happy and trying to make sure that everyone else was happy. I always wear Christmas sweaters, hats, glasses, and buttons to celebrate the season. It is also very important to me that we keep Jesus as the center of our holiday celebrations.

So you can see that we were just an ordinary family looking forward to an ordinary Christmas celebration together. *That, however, would not be the case. At least not this year.*

Your Insights & Reflections

What family traditions do you currently have or want to create in the future? What are the God-given gifts of each family member?

2

Odd Behavior

Jasmine and I had just finished leading the Toys for Tots distribution at our church. Toys for Tots is a program run by the United States Marine Corps Reserve which distributes toys to children whose parents cannot afford to buy them gifts for Christmas. The program was founded in 1947 by reservist Major Bill Hendricks. The idea behind the annual toy drive is that by providing kids with a toy we can deliver to them a message of hope. *We ourselves would be in need of hope sooner than we could have ever imagined.*

Together we had seen that every donated toy, bike, book, game, and doll had been sorted and picked up by parents. It was quite a feat to get everything done, but seeing the faces of the parents excited to be able to bring home all these toys to their children made all the long hours of work during the holidays worthwhile.

I noticed that Jasmine was not quite herself during the

toy distribution. She was a little irritable and sluggish. At seventeen, this behavior is not all that uncommon, but knowing Jasmine and how much she loves organizing and serving, I took note of her odd behavior. She said she had a headache and wasn't feeling well. I thought a lack of sleep along with the hectic holiday schedule was wearing on her so I just let her rest while we finished up at the church.

Gingerbread House

Later that evening, we began our annual Harris Gingerbread House Decorating Contest. This is always a very serious occasion. Jasmine inevitably has several tricks up her sleeve. The scene usually involves my middle child, Malcolm, eating more than he is decorating, his older brother, Eddie, putting forth a valiant effort to give Jasmine a run for her money, and me just enjoying the time with all my children. Yeah, right! I was laser focused on beating Jasmine this year. Daughter or not, the game was on!

Over the years, the boys became competitive because Jasmine and I would admire our work while teasing them about their "creation." She and I would have manicured lawns complete with snow flowers, perfect latticework across the roof, and beautiful icicles hanging from each edge. The boys would have a mess. But we all had fun!

We all tried to get Jasmine as a partner due to her exceptional creativity and decorating skills.

We decided to mix up the teams after a few years of totally shaming the boys. We all tried to get Jasmine as a partner due to her exceptional creativity and decorating skills. Conversely, we all tried to avoid Malcolm as a partner because he usually eats most of the candy and has been known to take a bite out of the house itself before the judging is complete.

But again, Jasmine was not her usual self—the one who effortlessly creates a gingerbread masterpiece while we struggle to keep ours from falling apart. This year Jasmine seemed out of it. She was a little quiet and left the kitchen early to go lie down. I wasn't too worried seeing that she had a headache earlier and thinking that she just needed to rest.

We finished up the gingerbread houses while she took a nap. Well, they were supposed to be houses, but the final result was up for debate. It just didn't seem the same without Jasmine's creative flair.

Thankfully Jasmine seemed to bounce back the next day as we celebrated Christmas Eve. We had fun watching our favorite Christmas movies and enjoying one of our favorite Harris family traditions—me burning Christmas cookies to a crisp! It happens every year without fail no matter what I try to do.

I have been an equal opportunity cookie burner, seeing that I've burned all kinds of cookies from basic sugar cookies to fancy turtle cookies. I've tried using the oven timer, staring at the cookies until they're done, and tying a string around my finger when I put the cookies in the oven. I've even tried praying not to burn the cookies! All to no avail. It seems store bought cookies will forever be our lot. *Two days later burnt cookies seemed like such a trivial problem.*

Finally, the big day was here, it was Christmas! Jasmine seemed about the same. She was a little low key, but nothing really out of the ordinary. We enjoyed a wonderful Christmas day, giving thanks for gifts that were shared while remembering the greatest gift of all—Jesus Christ.

The day after Christmas, Jasmine began to have a headache once again. She also complained about a little nausea so we thought she might be having some sinus issues and treated her accordingly. She felt a little better after taking the medicine.

Later that night, I had an eerie feeling, and out of the blue suggested we check Jasmine's blood pressure just in case it was elevated. I know, she was only seventeen years old, but I just felt like we should check it. Unfortunately, we could not find the blood pressure cuff, and it was late. We decided to continue our search in the morning if she still needed it or buy another cuff if we did not find it. She said that she felt better so we gave up the hunt for it. But she was not better.

Your Insights & Reflections

Have you ever felt a gentle nudge to do something out of the blue? Have you ever felt a strong urge to do something with urgency that seems to come out of nowhere?

_____
_____
_____
_____
_____
_____
_____
_____
_____
_____
_____
_____
_____
_____
_____
_____
_____
_____

3

Things Change in an Instant

December 27, 2012—the day that changed our lives forever.

I was awakened at 2:30 am by Jasmine calling out to me, "Ma!" in between episodes of projectile vomiting as she sat on the bathroom floor. I went in to help her and comfort her, thinking that either she had eaten something that upset her stomach or she had contracted some type of stomach bug. We stayed up for a while together until her stomach settled down. She said she felt better and went back to bed.

But she wasn't better. I am a light sleeper. Every time Jasmine got up to run to the bathroom, I got up too to make sure she was okay and help her in whatever way I could. She had five episodes of vomiting throughout the night, and by the third one I thought to myself, *Oh, that's it. She has a stomach virus. That's what was causing the headache. She will feel better in the morning.* I had no idea what would lie ahead in the coming hours.

In the morning my son Eddie and I went to the grocery store to pick up some crackers and ginger ale in an effort to soothe Jasmine's stomach. She was resting on the couch downstairs, and we told her that we would be right back. We quickly snatched up the groceries and headed right back to the house. We were three minutes from our front door when my cell phone rang. It was Jasmine. I said hello, and she responded with what sounded like baby talk!

She did not have a...virus. Jasmine, my beautiful baby girl, was having a stroke!

Suddenly all the pieces of the puzzle fell into place as non-coherent sounds echoed in my ear. Jasmine was not just tired; she did not have a sinus infection or a stomach virus. Jasmine, my beautiful baby girl, was having a stroke!

How did I know? A year previously, one of my dear friends had gone to the same grocery store after church, and she was chatting with a friend while shopping. All of a sudden she just stopped talking mid-conversation. The friend quickly jumped into action and alerted her husband, and she was rushed to the hospital.

It turned out that she had suffered a massive stroke, and her initial symptom was a loss of speech. I went to see her in the emergency room and prayed with her and her husband. I also spent time with her during her rehab and recovery and was very familiar with what she went through as a result of the stroke. Unfortunately her voice never came back, but to this day, she and I are still the best of friends. She calls me and although she can't say one audible word, we stay on the phone for an hour or more because as anyone who knows me will say, I love to talk. So when she calls, I've learned to ask questions and give her time to respond by making various sounds.

Because of how my friend could not speak when she had her stroke, when Jasmine called me with her slurred speech, I immediately thought of a stroke. Being that Jasmine was only seventeen, I would not have responded the way I did when she called if I had not recently experienced this situation with my friend.

I assured Jasmine that we were almost there and turned my attention to driving home as fast as I could. I began praying and pleading the healing blood of Jesus over my daughter. I sped into the driveway, telling my son to quickly get the groceries out of the car and call his dad. I sprinted up to the house and ran to the living room where Jasmine was resting when we left, but she was not there. Taking the stairs at a frantic pace, I hurried up to her room and found her lying on her bed. When I eased her up to a sitting position with my arm supporting her back, she was still mumbling gibberish. She looked dazed and confused, but I could see that she was crying out for help and trying to understand what was happening to her.

> Nothing, and I mean nothing, is more painful than seeing your child in desperate need of help and not being able to immediately make it all better. Nothing.

My mind was all over the place at that point. I thought, *Wait, how do you know it is a stroke? You're not a doctor. Her blood sugar could be low.* She was really limp and unstable so I dressed her as quickly as I could and called to Eddie to bring her a glass of orange juice, which is what we always had to do for my grandmother when she had low blood sugar episodes.

After I had her drink a few ounces of the orange juice, which didn't seem to help, I helped her downstairs and out to the car. The public service announcements warning that "every second counts" when it comes to a stroke were ingrained in my mind so I did not want to wait for an ambulance to come and transport her to the emergency room.

Signs and Symptoms of Stroke*

Knowing the signs and symptoms of a stroke is the first step to ensuring medical help is received immediately. For each minute a stroke goes untreated and blood flow to the brain continues to be blocked, a person loses about 1.9 million neurons.

This could mean that a person's speech, movement, memory, and so much more can be affected.

Learn as many stroke symptoms as possible so you can recognize stroke FAST and save a life! Stroke symptoms include:

• SUDDEN numbness or weakness of face, arm or leg, especially on one side of the body

• SUDDEN confusion, trouble speaking, or understanding

• SUDDEN trouble seeing in one or both eyes

• SUDDEN trouble walking, dizziness, loss of balance or coordination

• SUDDEN severe headache with no known cause

Call 911 immediately if you observe any of these symptoms. Note the time of the first symptom. This information is important and can affect treatment decisions.

*Source: National Stroke Assoc., www.stroke.org

Your Insights & Reflections

What is truly most important to you? How do you keep things in perspective when life is hectic?

_____
_____
_____
_____
_____
_____
_____
_____
_____
_____
_____
_____
_____
_____
_____
_____
_____
_____

4

Peace in the Midst of Crisis

I am recounting the story step by step, but this all took place in the space of about five to seven minutes from the time she first called me to the time we were in the car heading for the hospital. The Wake Med emergency room was eight minutes from our front door, but it took me only about five minutes to get there that day. I was driving down New Bern Avenue, heading towards the hospital and had just passed the nearby shopping center. We were about to cross the bridge that goes over the highway, when time stood still. It was literally like we were in a slow motion movie.

The sun illuminated the car and I felt really warm. I was driving well over seventy and probably more like eighty miles an hour, but time stood still and it felt like we were barely moving. I looked over at Jasmine slumped down in the passenger's seat. Having a medical background I could see that she was dying because I've sat with people who have died. I could literally see life leaving her body. The sun was shining directly on her face through the windshield, and my baby was dying. But I felt a peace permeate the atmosphere of the car. It was as though we were in another dimension.

> "God, I don't know if today is the day that you take my baby, but if it is, you are still good."

I said out loud in a calm, resolute voice, "God, I don't know if today is the day that you take my baby, but if it is, you are still good." When I said those words, the presence that I felt in the car became a presence inside me. It was like I had an overwhelming inner sense of peace, of release, of almost joy at such a tragic moment, as inexplicable as that sounds. I felt peace whether Jasmine was to live or die, whatever was to happen. *And from that moment, I continued to have a peace that truly does surpass all understanding.*

> *Be anxious for nothing, but in everything by prayer and supplication, with thanksgiving, let your requests be made known to God; and the peace of God, which surpasses all understanding, will guard your hearts and minds through Christ Jesus* (Philippians 4:6-7) KJV.

It seems odd to proclaim God's goodness in a time of tragedy, but that is exactly what happened. I take no glory for this because I know that I was operating on total Holy Ghost power at that point. There is no human strength, insight, intellect, or intestinal fortitude that can carry a person through a crisis like that. God was holding me and my daughter in his hands.

God is good just because of who he is, not necessarily what he has done for me. I didn't have any insight into whether she was going to live or die. And quite honestly, at that point, I thought she was dying. The testimony that I declared was that he was good based on my relationship with him already. If my daughter died, I said that he was still good regardless.

Therefore confess your sins to each other and pray for each other so that you may be healed. The prayer of a righteous person is powerful and effective (James 5:16) NIV.

I'd heard it said and even said myself that "You can't wait until you get into a situation to begin praying." You have to store up prayers in heaven and live a life of prayer. Pray without ceasing. No doubt, the prayer, praise, and worship that had gone up way before now were also sustaining me that day. (Of course, prayer is effective no matter how many times we have either prayed or not prayed before. God hears us no matter what.)

We were only on the bridge for a few seconds, but it seemed like an eternity. I know the Holy Spirit met me on that overpass and did just what God said he would do—he comforted me. Yes, the Comforter did come just as God promised. And he brought peace, love, and a blessed assurance that everything was going to be all right. The beautiful thing is that I was still under the impression that Jasmine was dying at this point.

This is not the praise, dance, and shout portion of this story. But it did forever change my perspective about death to one of knowing that God is in control of its timing. *God is good no matter what the ending of a crisis is.*

We crossed the overpass in short order and headed into the hospital parking lot. Jasmine was barely conscious. I got her into the ER and told the nurse that she needed to be seen immediately. Believe it or not, the nurse gave me a hard time. She went into the typical spiel about paperwork and insurance cards, and said the words she had probably said a thousand times before, "Please take a seat and we will be with you shortly."

I knew she was just doing her job, but a mother knows when her child is in extreme need of emergency help. I had wrestled Jasmine into a wheelchair at this point and was about to lose all the peace that I just received on the overpass. I loudly told the nurse that this was a dire emergency and Jasmine needed to be seen immediately. She insisted that I sit down and told me to be patient.

I defiantly told her, "I am not moving until they triage Jasmine." She finally listened to me and began to type. Then her fingers suddenly stopped keying in the information, and she shook her head and sighed. She looked up and informed me that I would still have to wait because the computers just went down. I pleaded with her but she held firm, saying that they could not do anything until the computers came back up.

Okay, this is the part where the story takes a turn. I got angry at her. Sorry, I know that doesn't sound like the Christian thing to do, but there is such a thing as righteous anger and boy did I have it that day! I didn't shout at her Rambo style, but I sternly demanded that they needed to see Jasmine immediately! I insisted that she have Jasmine's blood pressure checked because she was my daughter and I knew something was seriously wrong with her. I told her if Jasmine's blood pressure was normal, then and only then would I sit down. By then we had an audience because I was getting really loud, and people were trying to see what would happen next.

Another nurse offered to take Jasmine's blood pressure to deescalate the situation. I gratefully thanked her and she wheeled Jasmine to the triage room across the hall as I followed them. When she saw the results of Jasmine's blood pressure reading, a sheer look of terror came across her face. She called the doctors and nurses who ran in and rushed Jasmine to the back. By the time they got her into the room and onto the gurney, she was unresponsive. They were rubbing her sternum with their knuckles and shouting her name, trying to rouse her to respond.

I retreated to the corner out of the way and continued to lift Jasmine and the doctors up in prayer.

People were running around all over the place, in and out of the room. I retreated to the corner out of the way and continued to lift Jasmine and the doctors up in prayer. After the medical staff did some preliminary interventions, Jasmine finally opened her eyes and showed some signs of life. After lifting up a quick "Thank you," I resumed praying. The medical team quickly determined she needed an immediate CAT scan of her brain.

As they contacted the Radiology department and prepared to transport her there, the nurse looked at me praying in the corner and said, "We are just going to do a CAT scan to rule out any bad stuff. I'm sure everything is okay." But she wasn't sure, how could she be? She was just trying to be nice and for that I was grateful.

I walked as fast as I could beside the gurney, holding Jasmine's hand and praying as they whisked her down to Radiology. While they took her in for the scan, I paced back and forth, back and forth in the waiting room. At this point, my prayer changed; I was in full-blown intercession. Praying out loud, not caring what anyone thought, I began urgently talking to my God about my precious daughter and I declared the power of the almighty God to intervene on her behalf.

Just then, God spoke to me for the first time since this situation started. I felt an even deeper peace in the core of my being than I had felt when we were driving over the bridge. I heard an internal voice of assurance say, "She will live."

I responded out loud, "Okay, Father, thank you! She's gonna live!"

Your Insights & Reflections

Have you ever felt that God was speaking to you?

_____

_____

_____

_____

_____

_____

_____

_____

_____

_____

_____

5

Confidence

Suddenly I had 100% confidence that Jasmine was going to live because my heavenly Father had spoken to my heart. Hallelujah! It really didn't matter what the doctors or anyone else said at that point because I knew in my spirit that God had sealed her fate, and she was going to live.

Where does that level of confidence come from? How do we know that we have heard from God? It may be a little hard to imagine such assurance if we have not experienced a personal relationship with God.

There has been a great amount of debate regarding whether or not God speaks to us. And there has been even greater debate about how he speaks. My personal experience with God has centered around my ability to talk to him and to intently listen to what he says to me.

I've personally experienced God speaking to me in several ways. Sometimes God speaks through his word when I read scriptures relative to various situations in my life. Other times God sends people my way to share their experiences that help me know what God wants me to say or do. In this critical situation with my daughter, God spoke directly to me with a soft, inner voice of assurance.

Suddenly I had 100% confidence that Jasmine was going to live because my heavenly Father had spoken to my heart.

It would be a real injustice here not to also mention the need for us to act on the messages we receive from God. Our faith is activated by hearing the word of God as mentioned in Romans 10:17 "So then faith comes by hearing, and hearing by the word of God" (NKJV). But faith is an action word and we honor God by acting on the words that he speaks to us. While I haven't had any experiences that include an audible voice thundering down from heaven, God's ability to speak life changing messages to my heart has been no less impressive. Regardless how God has chosen to speak to me, I have always tried to listen and then act on his word.

Standing for what you know God has revealed to you in the face of opposition or circumstances that contradict what he has promised is not always easy. But we need to stand anyway. God is true to his word and he will keep his promises. And in this situation, I was depending on him to keep Jasmine alive. And it would not always be easy.

When they brought Jasmine out of the CAT scan and we headed back to the ER, no one said anything at first, but I could tell by the looks on their faces that the results were really bad. The chaplain was standing outside of Jasmine's room with a solemn look on his face. They had obviously called him to come and console me about the imminent death of my young daughter.

Diagnosis

The medical team once again gathered in her room and I learned that Jasmine had suffered a double threat—both a blood clot and a stroke at the same time. The physician described the blood clot as a massive one, covering most of the occipital region of Jasmine's brain and extending into her left jugular vein. I can't recall the exact words the medical team used, but the look on their faces is what struck me the most. Their solemn expressions, coupled with the gravity in their voices, drove home the critical nature of Jasmine's condition. The nurse who earlier told me she was sure that everything was all right gave me a big consoling hug after the doctor delivered the news. That meant a lot to me since I was still there all alone with my baby's life on the line.

> Their solemn expressions, coupled with the gravity in their voices, drove home the critical nature of Jasmine's condition.

The pediatrician on call instructed the team to intubate Jasmine and send her to Duke Children's Hospital for a higher level of care. While they were doing this procedure, the chaplain took me to the little quiet room where they take people when their loved ones are about to die in the hospital. He calmly asked me if I wanted some crackers or something to drink, but I politely declined. When he asked if he could get me anything else, I emphatically said, "Yes, you can print me off some healing scriptures." He looked puzzled and left the room. I guess he had never heard that request before.

When I returned to Jasmine's room, they had put her on life support and were preparing her for transport. By this time, my husband and my mother had arrived. They were both distraught, trying to come to grips with the harsh reality of seeing Jasmine lying there on a respirator.

The chaplain quickly returned with a print out of some healing scriptures. He handed me the paper as he greeted my husband and my mom. My husband and I embraced as we looked at our baby girl, wishing that we could trade places with her. We would do anything to see our Jazz well.

The nurse from the front desk who had insisted that I sit down and wait also came back and hugged me. I immediately reassured her that she couldn't have known the severity of Jasmine's condition and released her from any guilt that would try to bother her about our earlier interaction. There was no room for unforgiveness or anger in my heart when I needed to be in direct communion with my heavenly Father.

My mom and my husband went to the quiet room, and I began to recite the following healing scriptures over Jasmine while they finished prepping her.

> *My son, attend to my words; incline thine ear unto my sayings. Let them not depart from thine eyes; keep them in the midst of thine heart. For they are life unto those that find them, and health to all their flesh* (Proverbs 4:20-22) KJV.

This scripture helped me understand that God's word is more than words on a page. When mixed with faith, God's word in Scripture becomes medicine that brings health to those that believe. Speaking this verse aloud served as spiritual medicine for Jasmine.

> *Dear friend, I hope all is well with you and that you are as healthy in body as you are strong in spirit* (3 John 1:2) NLT.

This scripture assured me that God wants us to be healthy, and so I spoke good health over Jasmine.

> *I will not die; instead, I will live to tell what the LORD has done* (Psalm 118:17) NLT.

I spoke this verse as a declaration replacing "I" with "she" as I read it: "She will not die; instead she will live to tell what the Lord has done!"

Your Insights & Reflections

How has God's word impacted your life in times of crisis? What verses speak to where you are currently?

_____

_____

_____

_____

_____

_____

_____

_____

_____

_____

6

Comfort

As soon as the ambulance was ready, my husband and I climbed in with Jasmine and headed for Duke Children's Hospital. I'll never forget the thirty minute ride to Durham because I remember being surprised that they were not rushing and did not seem to drive in a hurry (at least that's the way it seemed to me at the time). There were no sirens blaring or lights flashing. It all appeared to reiterate the fact that they believed Jasmine was going to die, although I'm sure it was just standard protocol in the current traffic conditions.

When we arrived at Duke Children's Hospital, Jasmine was rushed to the Intensive Care Unit. I had called my church to have Jasmine put on the prayer list before we left the first hospital. We were not at Duke even five minutes before the counseling team of Pastors Dick and Lonnie from our church came to be with us. We had just joined that church a few weeks prior to this incident, and they were there with loving arms to support us. They prayed with us, made sure that we

Comfort

were fed, and most of all they just sat with us. As counseling pastors, they understood the importance of just being there for people in crisis.

Pastor Dick is a mature veteran who has known Christ for a long time. He has a practical way of looking at things and often shares encouragement in very simple terms, which meant so much to us. His wife, Lonnie, exuded a quiet strength that was very comforting to me. They stayed for over an hour and their presence spoke louder than any words they shared. They offered to do whatever they could to support us.

It can be challenging to find comforting words to say to others during times of crisis. Do you speak about the situation directly? Do you try to change the subject to get their minds off the current circumstance? Do you dare try to interject a well thought out glimmer of humor? Often times the best thing to say to someone in crisis is nothing. The strongest statement you can make is that you are there for them with your presence.

We all process grief, trials, and tragedy differently. The words that most resonated with me were hearing that God was with us. Everyone will go through difficult times and there is nothing more assuring than knowing that our heavenly Father is right there going through the situation with us.

God has said, "Never will I leave you; never will I forsake you" (Hebrews 13:5b) NIV. We talk a lot about trusting God and allowing him to have his way in our lives. Does this hold true in the possible loss of a child or a love one? Is God still God in tragedy and death? Is he truly sovereign? Is he still good? Choose to trust God. And yes, he is still good.

Your Insights & Reflections

7

Believe and Obey

The first day and a half of Jasmine's hospital stay at Duke are mostly a blur. I remember praying while reading the healing scriptures over her.

> *But he was wounded for our transgressions, he was bruised for our iniquities: the chastisement of our peace was upon him; and with his stripes we are healed* (Isaiah 53:5) KJV.

This scripture is very powerful as it paints the picture of Christ on the cross taking away all our sin, sickness, and disease. I read this scripture often to declare what Jesus had already done for Jasmine and that she had a right to health and healing because of Christ.

> *Pleasant words are as an honeycomb: sweet to the soul, and health to the bones. (Proverbs 16:24) KJV*

This verse supports the critical role that speaking the right words play in health and healing. There are no words better to say than those found in the Bible. I firmly believe that these scriptures are as powerful as any medicine when spoken in faith. The power is not only in the speaking but also in the believing. I had to believe what the Word said and eagerly anticipate the manifestation of healing in Jasmine's body.

> These scriptures are as powerful as any medicine when spoken in faith. The power is not only in the speaking but also in the believing.

Members of the medical team were constantly in and out of the room. They were also drawing Jasmine's blood frequently to monitor her anticoagulant (blood thinner) level. She remained on the respirator and was still unresponsive. I never left her side except to use the restroom that was located inside her hospital room.

My mom and my husband came to visit after work for a few hours each night. Eddie and Malcolm were unable to come see Jasmine due to the visitor restrictions in the intensive care unit. I called them nightly with updates and to check in to see how they were doing. They were a little numb like everyone else in the family. We all felt like we were in the middle of a nightmare. It's hard to put into words, but it's like we were awake and functioning while walking in a fog at the same time.

Even with mountain moving faith, it was hard to push past the reality of seeing Jasmine lying there on life support, completely unresponsive. I petitioned God in prayer and felt the urge to instruct the physicians to take her off the heavy medications that were keeping her so lethargic. I told them that it was time for her to wake up, but they told me the medicines were keeping her comfortable and would also prevent possible seizures. They explained that Jasmine had suffered a sub-clinical seizure during the past day and a half in the intensive care unit.

Second Day

The second day was a repeat of the first with the medical team in and out of the room often. Reality began to set in for all of us as we slowly came to grips with the fact that this was not a dream we would suddenly awake from like in the movies.

My husband's attention was split between work and Jasmine as he tried to keep busy. My mother was in the same situation, trying to balance work and coming down to Durham to see Jasmine. Eddie and Malcolm were still at home, getting ready to return to college from their holiday break.

We all continued with the same activities until the end of the second day when I felt God again urging me to have the doctors take Jasmine off all sedative medications. I felt like he was letting me know that it was time for Jasmine to wake up. I asked the nurse to call the physician and requested that Jasmine be taken off all sedative medications that could cause lethargy. The medical team thoroughly explained the potential risks and reluctantly honored my request.

Jasmine gradually regained consciousness and opened her eyes after two and a half days!

We were so thankful when Jasmine gradually regained consciousness and opened her eyes after two and a half days! It was the first time that her father and I had seen those beautiful brown eyes since this whole ordeal began, but she had the same confused and dazed look on her face that she had at home.

The physicians put additional precautions in place to monitor her brain activity and avert any potential seizures. It was a little nerve racking to tell a physician what to do in such a critical situation, but I had felt the prompting of the Holy Spirit to take her off the medicine so strongly that I had to obey. And now our baby was finally awake! Glory!

Your Insights & Reflections

What do you do when the Holy Spirit urges you to do something that defies human logic and reasoning?

8

All is Well

Sitting with Jasmine during the long hours in the hospital room, I had time to think back on my own experience with a crisis. I remembered some years earlier when I had a suspicious looking mole on the inside of my left ankle. The mole was dark with irregular borders, and it seemed to have changed in appearance from the first time that I noticed it.

I booked an appointment with my dermatologist to take a look at the mole to see if it needed to be removed. When my dermatologist examined it, he did not seem overly concerned. I asked him about risks for melanoma (skin cancer), and he said the relative risk for African-Americans is lower than fairer complexion individuals.

He told me that he was going to remove the mole and biopsy the tissue just to be sure. I began praying while he went to get his nurse to prep my ankle for the mole removal. The procedure was painful but tolerable. Later that week I was in prayer about the pending biopsy results and felt God's peace and heard my inner voice say, "All is well." I let out a sigh of relief. I didn't like to admit it, but I was a little worried.

The next day, I received a call from my dermatologist. I was glad to hear his voice and eagerly anticipated him saying that the biopsy results were back and everything was fine. But that is not what I heard. He said the results revealed some atypical cells and that I needed to come back in so that he could take more tissue from around the area to ensure he had removed it all.

Did I really hear from God or was that just wishful thinking? How do I know that I heard from God?

A flurry of questions flew through my mind: *What did you just say? Don't you know that God already told me that all is well? How is this possible seeing that I felt so strongly that God spoke to me about this issue? Did I really hear from God or was that just wishful thinking? How do I know that I heard from God?*

Just then, the same peace that had overtaken me when I prayed about the biopsy filled me again. I took a deep breath and set up a follow up appointment for the next day. I returned to his office and they removed the additional tissue. I had to take some time off work due to having a deeper wound than with the first biopsy.

During my recovery, several discouraging thoughts ran through my mind: *You must not have heard from God. This time it will come back as cancer.*

The Shunammite Woman

I kept countering those thoughts by repeating the words that I heard in my heart from my inner voice, "All is well. All is well. All is well." There was a battle going on in my mind for the next day or so until I heard the results from the second biopsy. I was able to keep my faith strong by reading the verses such as 2 Kings 4:26 aloud and not yield to the negative thoughts that would lead to my worrying about the situation.

> *Run at once to meet her and say to her, "Is all well with you? Is all well with your husband? Is all well with the child?" And she answered, "All is well"* (2 Kings 4:26) ESV.

This is a story about a Shunammite woman who was promised a son by a man of God. She did indeed have a son as he had said she would, but one day the young boy died. While on her way to find the man of God to tell him what had just happened, the man of God sent someone ahead to meet her and ask her if everything was all right with her, her husband, and her son. To which she replied, "All is well."

Her response raises several questions. Why would she

say all is well when her son was dead? And why didn't she tell him that her son had died? After meditating on that scripture and studying several commentaries, I understood that she declared, "All is well" because she knew everything would be all right. She knew that God was with her, and she kept her faith in God regardless of the trial that she was enduring at the moment.

I encourage you to obey God when you know that you are hearing clearly from Him.

God did heal her son and raise him to life again. He also blessed her and her family during a time of famine. The beauty of this story is that she did not wait until God healed her son or blessed her family to say, "All is well." She spoke in faith and taught a wonderful lesson for future generations to come.

I took the lesson of the Shunammite woman with me into my follow up appointment with my dermatologist. He told me that there were no cancer cells found in the second biopsy, and he was confident that he had gotten all the tissue he needed from the area around the border. Although I had made peace with whatever condition I might face that day, I was very relieved to hear the good news. Praise God!

Most importantly, I learned that all was not well because the biopsy was negative, but all was well because I knew Christ.

Thinking on this story reinforced my trust in God for Jasmine. Having the doctors take her off the sedatives is one of the many things I give God praise for because who knows how long she would have stayed in that unresponsive state with the constant heavy medication.

I encourage you to obey God when you know that you are hearing clearly from Him. It doesn't matter who or what challenges your faith. Believe God, take him at his word, and act accordingly.

Our baby was awake now, and we could begin the next phase of this difficult journey. Praise God!

Your Insights & Reflections

What are some of the experiences that you have had with God that you can draw strength from during challenging times?

_____
_____
_____
_____
_____
_____
_____
_____
_____
_____
_____
_____
_____
_____
_____
_____
_____
_____
_____
_____

9

Questions

If you have ever been around anyone with a brain injury or memory loss, then you have heard questions asked such as, What is your name? Do you know where you are? What is the date? Who is the president? Who is this?

Who is this? That is such a simple question, but it had a sobering impact on me when Jasmine could not answer that question as the doctor pointed at me. That experience evoked another series of questions for me. *What if she never recognizes her dad or me again? What happens to her memories? Why is this happening to her now when she is supposed to graduate high school in six months? Will she ever laugh again? Will she be in a vegetative state for the rest of her life? What about her wedding? Her children?*

I'm sure I know why some of those questions immediately came to mind—I was her mom. In that moment, I instantaneously began to lament the lost memories and lost potential for my baby girl. The mind can race far down the road in just a few seconds. Thank God for the Holy Spirit who again did what God said he would do—he brought the things to my remembrance that I needed in that moment.

> *But the Comforter, the Holy Spirit, whom the Father will send in my name, he shall teach you all things, and will bring to your remembrance all the things which I have said to you* (John 14:26) DARBY.

God had already told me that Jasmine was going to live. Now, I had to trust him for her recovery.

> ## God had already told me that Jasmine was going to live. Now, I had to trust him for her recovery.

Answers

Although Jasmine had finally awakened from her unresponsive state, she was not yet displaying signs of comprehension, speech, or mobility. The medical team ordered another CAT scan and MRI to see if there were any changes to the brain injury. Similar to the last experience in Radiology, I was pacing the floor praying while Jasmine underwent the diagnostic tests.

God spoke to my heart for the second time while Jasmine was in the MRI room. In the midst of my pacing, I felt a gentle inner voice say, "Total recovery, nothing missing, nothing broken." Again I responded out loud, "Thank you, Father, total recovery, nothing missing, nothing broken." It did not matter what the CAT scan, MRI, medical team, or anyone else said about Jasmine's prognosis. God had confirmed in my heart that Jasmine would have a full recovery!

It is always an interesting place to be when God has confirmed an answer to prayer in your heart, but the manifestation of what he said has not yet happened in the natural. It would be much easier if words that God has spoken to your heart were instantaneously followed up with miracles. That is just not how things work sometimes.

What do you do when God has spoken a word to your heart, but things have not changed in the natural?

What do you do when God has spoken a word to your heart, but things have not changed in the natural? What if things get worse? Did you really hear from God or was it just wishful thinking? Is God able to do what he said?

I hushed the voice of doubt with healing scriptures such as:

He sent out his word and healed them, snatching them from the door of death (Psalm 107:20) NLT.

God had already brought this verse to life for Jasmine. He had snatched her from the door of death and allowed her to live. Now we just had to keep the faith as she slowly progressed through her recovery. Surely a God that can save her from death is able to bless her with a full recovery. I was able to use the victory that had already been won to fuel my faith for future victories and hush the voice of doubt.

Hebrews 13:8 says:

Jesus Christ is the same yesterday and today and forever."
NIV

This scripture helped me stand firm in my belief that if God did it before, he can do it again.

Numbers 23:19 says:

God is not a man, so he does not lie. He is not human, so he does not change his mind. Has he ever spoken and failed to act? Has he ever promised and not carried it through?
NLT

This verse fortifies the fact that God does not change his mind about his word, and he will keep his promises.

Isaiah 55:11 says:

> *So will My word be which goes forth from My mouth; It will not return to Me empty, Without accomplishing what I desire, And without succeeding in the matter for which I sent it.* NASB

This verse is very comforting because it declares the absolute sovereignty of God's word. With reassurances like the ones found in these verses, there is no room for doubt.

My faith would be tested in the next couple of days as I boldly declared God's word regardless of how bleak things looked in reality. Jasmine was not showing any significant change in her cognition or mobility. In fact, she suffered a small set back due to some confusion with her blood thinning medication (anticoagulant), but I held on to God's word amidst uncertainty.

God answered my prayer when he said, "Total recovery, nothing missing, nothing broken." *Many times as believers all we have is a word from the Lord. Fortunately, a word from God is all we need.*

And as my grandmother would often say, "God said it, I believe it, and that settles it."

Your Insights & Reflections

What is your litmus test to confirm if God has spoken to you?
1. Does what you hear align with the Bible?
2. Will it bring glory to God?
3. Do you have a sense of peace about it?

_____
_____
_____
_____
_____
_____
_____
_____
_____
_____
_____
_____
_____
_____
_____
_____
_____

10

No One Gets the Glory but God!

The next day Jasmine spontaneously began to show remarkable improvements. She began to say a few words and she was more alert. My husband and I were overjoyed to see her take a turn for the better. She was also able to sip some ice chips and was eventually cleared for swallowing after a series of diagnostic tests. To the amazement of the medical team, Jasmine's body was coming into alignment with the word that God had released in my spirit. Jasmine had not received any new medications, medical procedures, or surgery. But right before our eyes she was miraculously improving, getting stronger and stronger as the hours passed.

> Right before our eyes she was miraculously improving, getting stronger and stronger...

Things were even a little comical as Jasmine tried to get anyone she could, including the housekeepers, to smuggle her some water after the intubation tube was removed. We explained that she had to wait for the physician's approval and she rolled her eyes. I remember thinking, *Oh yea, that's my Jazz, persistent as ever.* That was the first time my husband and I laughed since she arrived at the hospital.

There's nothing like seeing your God show himself mighty in a way where no one can get the glory but him.

It appeared that we had made it through the worst part of this trial after she was sent to a regular floor in the hospital and was later released to go home for outpatient rehab. It had only been eight days, but it felt like an eternity. God had taken Jasmine from death's door to being discharged from the hospital by performing a modern day miracle. There's nothing like seeing your God show himself mighty in a way where no one can get the glory but him. But that was not the end of our trials, in many ways it was just the beginning.

Believe and Obey Part 2

We were so blessed and relieved when we left Duke Children's hospital with our baby girl, but our story was far from over. Jasmine would need to begin outpatient rehabilitation and relearn the activities of daily living.

A few days afterwards, I received a call from one of the head physicians at Duke Children's hospital. She had been away during the holidays and had just returned from her vacation. Upon her return to the hospital, she reviewed Jasmine's medical record and could not understand how someone with a brain injury as serious as Jasmine's could be discharged without surgery or a medication to relieve intracranial pressure.

She explained her concern and said that she firmly believed that Jasmine's vision was at risk. I told her that Jasmine would not have surgery or any additional medication because God had already healed her. She went on to explain that Jasmine had not received a shunt or medication to relieve the pressure caused by her brain injury, which if left untreated could lead to blindness.

I stood my ground and held firm to my position because God had confirmed his word that Jasmine was healed. The doctor continued to plead with me that there was no medical intervention done that could have led to that type of injury spontaneously healing. I communicated my appreciation and respect her medical expertise, but I was not going to bring Jasmine back for further treatment. She was very concerned so

I offered to bring Jasmine to her for an evaluation only so that she could see for herself that God had miraculously healed her.

To the credit of the physician, she was on vacation during Jasmine's hospitalization and had not physically seen her. She had only reviewed her medical record and it just did not make sense to her based on her medical knowledge.

Although I was quite firm on the phone, it was a little nerve-racking after I hung up with her when thoughts came that demanded, "Who do you think you are, you're not a physician!" To which I answered out loud, "True, I'm not a physician. But I know the great physician and he already healed Jasmine!"

Okay, God

We went back to Duke Children's hospital to see the physician as agreed. Fleeing thoughts of doubt tried my faith. "What if she sees something on the exam? What if I'm wrong and did not hear God clearly?" I hushed the voice of doubt with healing scriptures, and praised my heavenly Father for his miraculous healing power.

We arrived at the office and the physician took Jasmine back for the exam. I joined them in the room and sat quietly reading my *Prayers That Bring Healing* book by John Eckhardt. While I'd like to say that my faith was rock solid and I had complete confidence that the exam would be negative, that's just not the case. I was shaking in my boots! I was praying in the Spirit, reading the healing scriptures, and pleading the blood of Jesus. There was some serious spiritual warfare going on in that exam room!

> "Okay, God, I stood on your word and went against the doctor's recommendations.... I need you to back me up."

I said in a whisper, "Okay, God, I stood on your word and went against the doctor's recommendations. I told her you healed Jasmine miraculously and she did not need surgery or any additional medication to relieve the intracranial pressure. I need you to back me up. In Jesus' name, amen."

Just then, the physician leaned back in her chair and stared at Jasmine in amazement. She said to her, "Your mom has good prayer."

I replied, "No, her mom has a good God." Of course, I had a little swag in my reply like *Yep, that's what my God can do!*

Truth is, I was so relieved inside! I was thinking, *Whew, my God did it again.* It would have looked really bad to have this physician discredit what had been proclaimed as a miracle from God, especially given her different opinion on the role of faith in medical treatment decisions.

Your Insights & Reflections

What are some of the ways that God has worked in your life in which no one can get the glory but him?

11

Rehab

The rehabilitation process was quite the experience for Jasmine. I had taken family leave from my job and never left her side since she first had the stroke. My husband and my mom were both working so they were not able to attend the rehabilitation appointments that were scheduled during normal business hours. Eddie and Malcolm were away at college and had to keep up with what was going on over the phone. And so rehab was something Jasmine and I shared.

    I do have medical experience in my background and had spent a good deal of time taking care of my grandparents so caregiving was not something new to me. I spent a lot of time with my grandmother who was the matriarch of the family, a woman of God, a woman of prayer. I was introduced to Christ through my grandmother. I went to be with my grandparents because my grandfather was disabled and my grandmother's health was failing due to complications of diabetes.

> She was the one who introduced me not only to knowing about Christ, but what it really means to be the hands and feet of Christ.

My grandmother had helped to purchase the church building; it was in her family. There was a preacher there who was the pastor of the church, but my grandmother was like the caregiver. We would arrive early and light a piece of paper to get the pilot light going to keep the church heated. She was the one who introduced me not only to knowing about Christ, but what it really means to be the hands and feet of Christ. So I've always seen my relationship with Christ to be not only the receiving of the gift of salvation, but also understanding that with that gift comes a responsibility to help serve and be the hands and feet of Christ to others.

So my experience very early was actually caring for the church, caring for my brothers and sisters in Christ, through watching her humanitarian efforts. For instance there was her desire to help children attend church so she bought a van and my uncle went to a salvage yard and tore out the seats of school buses and bolted them down in the van. I painted the side of the van with the name of the church. And we would take corn beef hash and peanut butter and jelly sandwiches to the kids and I would teach them Vacation Bible School lessons. Through all of that, I gleaned from my grandmother. Church wasn't a building to me—we were the church, the living church.

My grandfather used to drive a truck, but after his health deteriorated, he could no longer work. My grandmother provided nursing care for awhile in Pinehurst, which is near where we lived. She was a nurse's aid in a nursing home for quite some time.

As they got older I spent time taking care of my grandparents, serving them as my grandmother had served the church, and giving back to her all the care she had bestowed on others. I took care of them by just being there if they were to fall, and trying my best to get my grandmother to be compliant to take her meds and eat better, but I never won that battle.

My grandfather had zero muscle strength and he would drag his feet along the floor. He couldn't lift anything. If he were to fall or bend over, he couldn't straighten himself. Unfortunately, he would fall at times and I would have to get my body under him to help him stand. When he was seated with his legs at a 90 degree angle, all of us, myself and any other adults around, would have to grab him by the belt and lift him up. So he had a major physical disability with its accompanying lack of mobility.

My grandmother was a chronic diabetic and had typical health issues associated with being overweight and not eating a good diet. She was the best southern cook in the world, but she would have bouts of high and low blood sugar. Sometimes she would be incoherent because her blood sugar was so bad after eating something she shouldn't have. Unfortunately it got to the point where she too would have falls from time to time due to black outs. She even had a couple close calls with driving. So my living with them was literally like giving them home health care.

Caring for Others

Because I loved caring for folks in general, my grandmother recommended that I enter the medical field. After taking care of my grandparents, I studied radiology for two years and then became a medical assistant to a physician for thirteen years. So I have some understanding of what rehab is all about. But walking through the door of the rehab center with my daughter at the tender age of seventeen was a surreal experience.

God would indeed have to help us through the process.

Your Insights & Reflections

12

The Process

I've assisted wheelchair bound patients but never was in a position of helping my own child with rehab. Just getting her out of the car and helping her into the center took forever. People were looking at her since this was a brain injury and stroke rehab center, and most everyone going there was over 60 and she was just 17 years old.

I'm sure she was not the first young person to have that happen to her, but even the nurses were curious, probably wondering why someone so young and pretty was there. No one could explain why this happened to Jasmine, but that was not important. Our focus was on helping her through this stage of her recovery.

We did everything we could to shield Jasmine from the harshness of what had happened until she went to rehab. At that point she didn't grasp all that had transpired because she didn't remember it. We hadn't yet sat her down and told her all the details.

So going to the rehab center was the first time she had to come to grips with the reality of her stroke. Jasmine's first couple of rehabilitation appointments were quite challenging since she was forced to deal with her current condition.

They tested her abilities and set goals for the duration of her rehabilitation, which is what made those first couple of visits so hard. In the beginning they did an assessment to get a baseline to determine the progress of each therapy session. They wanted to see how many steps she could initially walk, if she could go up stairs, what daily activities she could perform, and if she could pronounce difficult words so they could assess any speech impediments.

> She had to say, "Wait a minute, I don't know how to walk up the stairs."

In the beginning they took her over to three little steps to see if she could climb them. They have apparatus that are like obstacle courses to test the patient. It was hard because that was the first time she had to say, "Wait a minute, I don't know how to walk up the stairs." Later with the speech therapist she was also forced to admit, "Wait a minute I don't know how to say this." When the lady asked her questions like what is 2 + 4, she had to laugh at her own inability.

They began forcing her to try to process things. They would say things like, "I'm going to say a word to you—'pin.' I need you to remember that word." And they would ask her what they just said and she would be able to answer "pin." But they would say something else to her and then again ask her, "What is the word I asked you to remember?" and she couldn't do it.

All those things were exposing how much mental and physical dexterity she had lost and where she was with her brain function and her physical fitness. As a mom, watching her not be able to do so many easy activities and seeing her go through that period of realizing that she couldn't do them were extremely difficult.

The testing revealed all that she could and could not do. That was painful to watch and hard for her to deal with. I remember her saying things like: "I didn't even think about not being able to walk up stairs." At home, she didn't have to worry about things like that because we had converted our living room on the first floor into her rehabilitation suite. We both slept downstairs and she received the same level of care at home that she had gotten in the hospital.

I was concerned about her ability to emotionally and physically handle all that was happening to her. That was a lot for a 17 year old kid to have to shoulder. To deal with it all, I prayed in the Spirit a lot and read lots of healing scriptures, such as, "He [God] will never leave you nor forsake you" (Deut. 31:6 NIV) and "My strength is made perfect in weakness" (2 Cor. 12:9) NKJV.

I surrounded us with worship music playing 24/7 and not only read the Word, but kept the Word audibly playing on DVDs and CDs. Like I said, we took over the whole bottom floor for her and we kept the CD player on so that the Word was playing in our ears and we could just really draw close into God. His Word is life. The Spirit alone gives eternal life. Human effort accomplishes nothing. The very words he speaks to us are spirit and life.

I kept the CD player on so that the Word was playing in our ears and we could just really draw close into God.

I couldn't get caught up with what the doctors were saying, what things she couldn't articulate, or what steps she couldn't take. I couldn't focus on the doctor's report, I had to focus on my heavenly Father's report. We played contemporary songs such as "Our God Is an Awesome God" and all the good old hymns such as "Amazing Grace." Songs that talked about him, his power, his ability, and his sovereignty were the most comforting.

And do not be drunk with wine, in which is dissipation; but be filled with the Spirit, speaking to one another in psalms and hymns and spiritual songs, singing and making melody in your heart to the Lord, giving thanks always for all things to God the Father in the name of our Lord Jesus Christ (Ephesians 5:18-20) NKJV.

The hardest part of the rehabilitation process was Jasmine's anticoagulant therapy. I had to give her injections twice a day, and she hates needles! This was hard on both of us because I hated to do it, knowing that it caused her so much anxiety. She admitted that the needle or the injection itself was not really painful. It was just the thought and anticipation of having to get a shot. It was rough but we got through it with God's help.

Your Insights & Reflections

How do you create an environment where your faith is revived during trials and challenges? Which songs stir your spirit to press on in the faith?

13

Progress Begins

The staff at the outpatient site were very friendly and demonstrated a high level of patience with Jasmine. She slowly began to show progress with walking, speech, and cognition. They conducted exercises to help her with her memory and processing speed as well.

From the beginning of week two into week three, she started to show some progress both physically and emotionally because she kind of understood what the process was. Like anything else, if you do something enough times, you will begin to understand what is expected of you. So she began to show some progress with her walking and stairs. Because they had a little track, not even a quarter of a mile long, right outside of her room, I would walk that track while they were doing things in the treatment room with her and then they would walk her out and around the track.

The first time she only went a few feet or so before she needed the wheelchair, and then the next time, they would encourage her to go a little ways more. So it went from a few feet until she could do a few yards, and then she would do a quarter of the lap around, then she did a half, and then she could do a full circle. After she could do the full circle, they would say, "Now that you can do a full circle, let's do a few stairs." Then a day or two later, "Now that you can do the stairs, let's do the full circle, some stairs, and let's go outside for a few steps."

So it wasn't just always more of the same. They would progressively add another level of activity including: stepping off a curb, doing a few stairs, and going outside. They were very thorough in their approach to her rehabilitation.

From the beginning of week two into week three, she started to show some progress both physically and emotionally.

They gave us little exercises to do at home along with homework that was level appropriate for where she was with her cognitive ability.

Sitting in on the rehab sessions help me understand how to reinforce her learning between appointments. Jasmine was 17 years old and six months away from graduating high school when this all began. Would she ever make it there? At first she could not process even the concept of it.

Progress Begins

I just held onto the word God had said, "Total recovery, nothing missing, nothing broken."

It is like in the movie *Men in Black* where the guy flashes people with a device and they lose their memory about an incident. Those memories were gone but not forever. I just held onto the word God had said, "Total recovery, nothing missing, nothing broken." I knew that meant she was going to be able to graduate with her class and go to college.

At first we were at home with elementary school level workbooks reintroducing Jasmine to the basics of reading and writing. That was a pill that was extremely hard to swallow for Jasmine and the entire family.

I bought simple coloring books for hand eye coordination and fine motor skills. Simple word find puzzles and word association tablets helped with her processing skills. She was a trooper but I could tell that the simplicity of the exercises bothered her at times.

She had always liked to stay busy as a child, so relearning things kept her occupied now. When she was little, if she was near any paper, she would tear it up and make little purses and things. We sowed into her gift because we saw it early. So she would have friends over and they made jewelry. She enjoyed crocheting, knitting, and sewing, pretty much anything she could do with her hands. So her natural bent toward making things helped her now because she was in the process of remaking her life.

And Moses said to the children of Israel, "See, the Lord has called by name Bezalel...and He has filled him with the Spirit of God, in wisdom and understanding, in knowledge and all manner of workmanship, to design artistic works, to work in gold and silver and bronze, in cutting jewels for setting, in carving wood, and to work in all manner of artistic workmanship (Exodus 35:30-33) NKJV.

Progress Begins

Your Insights & Reflections

What is one area of your life where things may not be all that you would like them to be, but you recognize that there is progress?

_____
_____
_____
_____
_____
_____
_____
_____
_____
_____
_____
_____
_____
_____
_____
_____

14

Resuming School

The days turned into weeks and the weeks turned into two and a half months. Jasmine began to show tremendous progress throughout her rehabilitation process. She regained strength and functionality rapidly after the first few weeks of therapy. But high school graduation? Was that even possible with all the school she had missed? We had to go to the school and apply for her reinstatement.

She had been out for quite a while. We had to let them know what happened, show doctor's notes, and ask for special conditions so she could finish out her school year. I said that I would do what I could to teach her at home because I was not going anywhere until she was able to go back to school.

The school system at first flatly said no. They wanted to let her recover for the rest of the school year and decided she could redo her senior year. I said, "No, that doesn't allow for what God said, 'Total recovery, nothing missing, nothing broken.' Just tell me what we need to do for her to be able to graduate."

So after a pretty lengthy fight with them about that, they agreed to send work home and she would have to do tests online. Now at this point I thought, *Here I am again fighting this fight and she can't even remember 2 + 4.* That's why I talk about just standing on God's word. Finally I got the permission, and they sent the work home.

She was still working through her rehab, but towards the end of the rehab she was really coming back to herself. She was regaining more memories, and we were able to begin working through some of the homework they were sending. Her hardest struggle was recall. Because of the recall, math was very hard and reading comprehension was difficult too. If she read something in its entirety and then you asked her something about what she read five or ten minutes later, she could easily forget it.

Her first day back at school was as she puts it, "weird." Classmates who didn't know her well kept asking her what had happened and she really didn't know how to begin. One even said, "I heard you were dead." So that was stressful for her. When she did get comfortable enough to tell people what happened, some of them thought she was lying. It was hard for them to understand how she could have a stroke because most people associate that with someone who is older.

God, however, miraculously healed her, and she went from a low baseline and starting point to the place where she could handle what the school was sending home. She would have assignments that she needed to do herself and also have online assessments. For her midterms and finals, I had to drive her to school and she took them there. The outpatient nurses and the medical team worked with the school to tell them how she could be tested because when it got to her midterms, she wasn't ready to look at her paper, read, comprehend, and write an answer. She had to have her midterms given orally.

She had already had some extra credit before her stroke so thankfully she only had to finish two classes to meet the minimum graduation requirement. She only had two classes but that was a lot for her given her situation. But God blessed us—we have a beautiful Christian principal there at Millbrook High School and they rallied support for her and made it happen, and that's how she was able to graduate.

Your Insights & Reflections

How do you respond when people doubt your testimony or what God has done in your life?

15

Graduation Day

On the day of her graduation she was honestly in disbelief that it was really happening. As she describes it, "I was very grateful. I thought, *God is truly blessing me; He really has His hand on my life.* When we waited in line for our diplomas, I looked over at my guidance counselor who had told me that I should retake my senior year. When I returned to school he had said, 'You are definitely not going to graduate and definitely not going to college.' He had been so wrong. Only a few weeks after my graduation I was packing up for college."

Before this happened, she was thinking about going to a four year institution and majoring in Psychology. Afterwards with everything going on with cognitive issues, she decided to pursue her passion—working with creative things—which is why she went to the Art Institute to pursue fashion, marketing, and merchandising.

Jasmine explains, "Originally I wanted to major in Psychology because I felt like my calling was to help people who go through challenging situations. I was the friend that everyone called and told their problems. A lot of people used to tell me that I needed to be a guidance counselor. I enjoy supporting, encouraging, and motivating people, so originally I wanted to do that. Then I realized my true passion is for fashion, and I discovered that being an image consultant and a personal stylist is basically a combination of my two passions: psychology and fashion. You still get the chance to encourage people and help them with their overall image, while maintaining your ability to express your creativity."

After her graduation ceremony, which meant so much to her, Jasmine's friends wanted to party and have a good time, but she decided to go home and start packing since she would leave in two weeks for college. She started assembling what she would need and proceeded to do all the shopping for items she would use in her new apartment in Charlotte.

The day we drove her to Charlotte was momentous for all of us. When we turned into the apartment complex that would become her home during her college years, everything suddenly became real for all of us.

Jasmine had come a long way. She was indeed embarking on a new adventure. God had not only given her life back to her and us, he had given her a new part of the journey with "Total recovery, nothing missing, nothing broken." And yes, God was still good.

Your Insights & Reflections

What has God done in your life or in the life of someone you know that demonstrates his miraculous power?

_____
_____
_____
_____
_____
_____
_____
_____
_____
_____
_____
_____
_____
_____
_____
_____
_____
_____

Epilogue

If you haven't already, you will encounter situations where you have to choose either to stand on God's word as I did, or go with what others say about a matter. Always choose to believe God regardless of what the current circumstances dictate. Just say, "Okay, God, I'm stepping out on your word and I need you to back me up!" He will honor his word.

    The goodness of knowing Christ, the ability to be redeemed from sin, just the sheer fact of being unworthy and separated from him and then have his forgiveness and love is overwhelmingly awesome. He's good because of who he is, not necessarily what he has done for us. Some people have a hard time saying he is good when bad things happen, particularly with the loss of a child, which was what was staring me in the face.

    I didn't know that Jasmine was going to live at first. My testimony is that he is still good because what makes him good is not based on the circumstances in my life. He's good regardless.

This experience changed all of us in every way. We all have thought or said, "Life could change in a second. We are just one phone call away or one knock on the door away from a life changing moment." We know that, but until you are the one who picks up the phone, or the one who opens that door to the news, you just don't have the appreciation for what that really means. I may not have always done it that well, but that's one of the things I tried to communicate through this book. Everything you think to be important right now may not be important in the next few seconds. We say, "I've got to pay this bill…I've got to meet this deadline…I've got to catch this flight…I've gotta, I've gotta, I've gotta…"

Everything you think to be important right now may not be important in the next few seconds.

However, something can happen in your life where it just is not important anymore, and that's how it changed us. We all embrace life a little differently; we appreciate the fragility of life. We try to treat people with love and respect because we don't know if it's the last time we will see them. We are not perfect and still have times where we argue and complain—we are human after all—but we do have that heightened awareness of how quickly everything can change.

Epilogue

How do you know what your life will be like tomorrow? Your life is like the morning fog— it's here a little while, then it's gone (James 4:14) NLT.

But God remains the same. And he is still good.

Your Insights & Reflections

What would you do if you knew that you only had a short time to live?
What shifts would take place in your current priorities?
Why wait for bad news to make those changes?

_____
_____
_____
_____
_____
_____
_____
_____
_____
_____
_____
_____
_____
_____
_____
_____

Lessons Learned

Things that seem vitally important can become completely insignificant in an instant.

Everything that was happening in my life came to an abrupt halt when Jasmine suffered the stroke. Responsibilities at work, commitments at church, duties at home—everything stopped immediately. Cares and worries I had just a few seconds before Jasmine called me unable to speak became distant thoughts to be remembered no more.

You can have peace even in the midst of tragedy.

The peace that is promised in Philippians 4:7 is available to all of God's children. His peace truly does transcend all understanding.

Only God can give a mother peace when she is watching her child at the brink of death.

Your faith will be tested.

You may have mountain-moving faith, but your faith will still be tested. There is no reason to be ashamed because it only strengthens your relationship with God when you step out on faith and he backs you up.

Even the members of the "Faith Hall of Fame" in Hebrews 11 had moments when conflicting thoughts and circumstances tried their faith.

Sometimes there is a process that follows revelation.

God may reveal his will to you and still allow you to go through a process before the manifestation of what he said. God assured me that Jasmine would have a "Total recovery, nothing missing, nothing broken." But we still had to go through the outpatient rehabilitation process.

She had good days and bad days on her path to recovery. God was still good and his promise was sure on all of them.

> **Accepting Jesus Christ is the best
> decision you can ever make.**

This experience validated the value of having a relationship with my Lord and Savior Jesus Christ. The very essence of my being is rooted in my faith. There is no way that I could have made it through this trial without God. He made all of heaven's resources available to me and my family to help us persevere.

> **You are never alone.**

See, I am sending an angel before you to protect you on your journey and lead you safely to the place I have prepared for you (Exodus 23:20) NLT

The angel of the LORD encamps around those who fear Him, and he delivers them (Psalm 34:7) NIV.

Surely goodness and mercy shall follow me all the days of my life, and I shall dwell in the house of the LORD forever (Psalm 23:6) ESV.

God will never leave you.

The LORD himself goes before you and will be with you; he will never leave you nor forsake you. Do not be afraid; he will never leave you nor forsake you. Do not be afraid: do not be discouraged (Deuteronomy 31:8) NIV.

Your Insights & Reflections

After reading this book, what are the one or two things you will take forward with you in your walk with the Lord?

_____
_____
_____
_____
_____
_____
_____
_____
_____
_____
_____
_____

About the Author

With inspiring passion and courage, La'Wana Harris is committed to helping others achieve their potential. She is a certified energy management coach who thrives on seeing others maximize their potential. Driven by her firm belief in honoring and speaking truth, La'Wana is a dynamic facilitator gifted in creating conversations. Her pragmatic expertise in aligning people performance with business strategy has created a healthy career anchored by a broad base of professional experience. Her industry experience includes people and leadership development, training and facilitation, diversity and inclusion, people leadership and project management. She received her B.S. in Biology from Greensboro College.

La'Wana has also authored two children's book series. Her inspiration for the *Jaden Israel* book series is her grandson, Jaden Israel. Her books capture the journey of a little boy on the path to discovering and becoming the one God created him to be. Each story is based on sound biblical principles with supporting application tools. La'Wana is committed to protecting the innocence, imagination, and integrity of the next generation.

She recently launched her latest book series, *America by Train*, which combines her love for America and her fascination with trains. Her books capture the history and beauty found only by traveling America by train. Each story is complemented with activities to help readers create their own adventure. La'Wana is committed to igniting the imagination of the next generation of train enthusiasts.

La'Wana has also done missionary work in Haiti. She has conducted numerous mission trips there, focusing on providing mobile medical clinics, building orphanages, childrens ministry, evangelism and public health education. Her mission work is also demonstrated domestically through community revitalization and social justice projects.

But above all, La'Wana feels that her greatest accomplishments are being married to her high school sweetheart for 26 years, raising three healthy children, spoiling an adorable grandson, and accepting Christ as her Lord and Savior. Her faith and family shape the essence of her being.

www.ingramcontent.com/pod-product-compliance
Lightning Source LLC
Chambersburg PA
CBHW070544300426
44113CB00011B/1789